THE BEAUTY
of HOME

MARIE FLANIGAN

THE BEAUTY
of HOME

REDEFINING TRADITIONAL INTERIORS

TEXT WITH SUSAN SULLY
PHOTOGRAPHY BY JULIE SOEFER

GIBBS SMITH
TO ENRICH AND INSPIRE HUMANKIND

PREVIOUS: Barrel-back chairs, a stone table, and a metal-and-leather footstool atop a palomino rug forge a rich, textural palette. RIGHT: In a monochromatic composition, glass and metallic surfaces offer highlights against the matte textures of a fluted plaster table and slubby, silk-weave chairs. NEXT: Reflectivity reigns in a kitchen corner appointed with quartzite slab countertops, polished nickel hardware, and unlacquered-brass plumbing fixtures.

First Edition
24 23 22 21 20   5 4 3 2

Text © 2020 Marie Flanigan
Photography © 2020 Julie Soefer, except pages 28, 74, 207–213 © Claudia Casbarian,
pages 145 (right), 148 (right), 185, and 231 © Rachel Manning
Styling by Jessica Brinkert Holtam

Published by
Gibbs Smith
P.O. Box 667
Layton, Utah 84041
1.800.835.4993 orders
www.gibbs-smith.com

Designed by Jan Derevjanik
Printed and bound in China
Gibbs Smith books are printed on either recycled, 100% post-consumer waste, FSC-certified papers or on paper produced from sustainable PEFC-certified forest/controlled wood source. Learn more at www.pefc.org.

Library of Congress Control Number: 2020933149

ISBN: 978-1-4236-5466-7

TO JOE, JOHN, WILLIAM & EVE

CONTENTS

In the small Texas town where I grew up, values were less about possessions and more about family, community, and nurturing the well-being of neighbors and friends. Because my father truly cared about cultivating his children's passions and interests, he frequently took me to our local gallery where we spent Saturday afternoons looking at works of art with ritual bottles of cream soda in hand. I knew at a young age that I wanted to be an artist—assuming that meant becoming a painter. My mother, who extended her hand to everyone who came to our door, fostered my love of hospitality. She believed that a home should embrace the people within it, and through simplicity and kindness made even strangers feel welcomed. On holidays, she never rested until a bountiful meal was cooked, all the details were in place, and the table was dressed to perfection. From her, I learned the importance of composing a home for beauty and of preparing a place for the ease and enjoyment of all who come within its walls.

Early on in my life, I realized how powerfully beautiful spaces affected me and wanted to learn the rules and tools with which to bring that beauty into my own life. Fascinated by the idea of creating a work of art in which to live, I found my way to studying architecture. I was intrigued to discover the systems and structural theory surrounding this intrinsically creative discipline. As I learned the history of architecture, I was drawn equally to the orderly beauty of classical design and to the sculptural simplicity of modernism. Over time, I discovered that the lessons of these two schools could be joined to create timeless environments that meld the past with the present.

When I studied architecture in my twenties in the ancient Tuscan town of Castiglion Fiorentino, my life unfolded amid an antique cityscape. I was captivated by centuries-old buildings of limestone, brick, and travertine marble that seemed to bleed into one another beneath a sea of terra-cotta rooflines. The result was at once minimalist and satisfyingly sensual. These modest structures shared streetscapes with Renaissance and Baroque churches and monuments characterized by orderly grandeur and symmetrical adornment. Just by walking down the street, I discovered how disparate expressions of architecture—the simple and the grand, the vernacular and the classical—could coexist in a unified setting that was simultaneously grounding and elevating. I also learned that the rules of classical design are universal and that once you absorb them, you can bend and break them in innovative ways, reaching back through centuries to bring forward what is lasting and beautiful.

After working for several years in architecture, I journeyed into interior design. I found that I needed to work holistically and not stop when the architectural envelope was complete. Architecture begins a conversation that interiors carry out, which is why I value integrating the two. Memorable interiors do not rely on furniture and decor alone—they are created through a dialogue that takes place between the architecture of the space and the design elements that exist within it. My approach is to tap the mindset of an architect and the methodology of an interior designer in order to make a million calculations, both small and large, to arrive at a harmonious whole. I keep drilling down to the details, from the treatment of a wall—whether paneled or plastered, painted or papered—and the choice of lighting—a dramatic chandelier or a modern pendant—to all the contents in a room. Throughout the process, I am always aware of how my roots and education in architecture color my design decisions.

My work is about making meaningful connections, not only between architecture and interiors, but also among the home and the people living in it and all the tangible and intangible ingredients that compose an eloquent environment. The list of elements that can be joined in effective ways is infinite: volume and form, light and shadow, the natural and the man-made, the rough and the finished, color and its absence. These relationships can be tactile, as in a table I discovered made from the root of a natural teak tree. Hand-planed, the wood revealed swirling striations that posed an organic counterpoint to the table's sleek, geometric form. Another way to forge connections is through storytelling—fashioning narratives that celebrate the members of a family and their cherished possessions. One couple I worked with wished to blend the cultures of their Iranian and Korean families through the design of their home. By combining works by artists from both countries, fabrics that paid homage to their heritage, and important family pieces, including a Korean tea set that accented their living room, I was able to forge an environment that reflected the marriage of these two cultures.

I believe that home is more of an experience than a place. It encompasses the rooms that shape and bear witness to our lives. It is the haven we come back to each day. When thoughtfully articulated, it brings renewed life to all who enter. Intrinsically, our hearts seek beauty because it sparks hope, life, aspiration, and possibility. It has the power to transform. My goal as a designer is to bring more beauty into the world by changing the way the people I serve see life

or themselves, clarifying their vision of home and then bringing that to fruition. Every home should be replete with aesthetic pleasure, but it also needs to speak on emotional and spiritual planes in order to meet our most profound needs. By helping people discover what spaces feel intimately and uniquely theirs, I hope to elevate their experience and their journey.

Each home I design stands alone as an individual creation, but all share an unmistakable thread. This strand weaves throughout the components of design that define my work and are the tools of my craft: architecture,

composition, character, palette, illumination, detail, simplicity, depth, and surprise. In this book, I walk through each one of these components, sharing insights into their principles and applications. These are the building blocks of an environment that satisfies the senses and inspires the soul. From the magnificence of a vaulted ceiling to the delicacy of the most intricate trim, they address every part and piece of the house in a way that celebrates the vibrancy, vision, and values of those who dwell within. My hope is that this book will help you uncover the beauty in your life and your surroundings and to share that beauty with others.

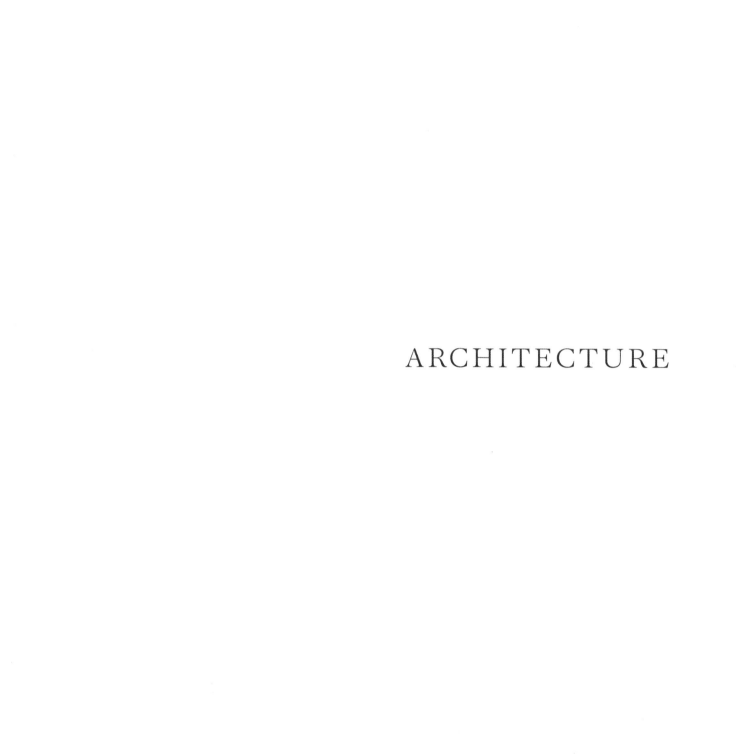

ARCHITECTURE

When architecture and interior design are considered together, they elevate one another. Architecture provides order and proportion. Interior design is what touches you, envelops you, and engages the senses. The most intimate discipline involved in building, it takes a structure and brings it to life. People often assume interior design is just about putting things on top of an existing framework. In actuality, it is most powerful when you work in the opposite order, starting with the building blocks of form, material, and light, then adding layers slowly with intention and restraint. By the time you get to the finishing touches associated with decorating—upholstery, drapery, rugs—you will have created a holistic environment that promotes comfort and delight.

I prefer to work with the architect from the beginning of a project, combining our different perspectives in a synergistic way. This allows me to become immersed in the architectural vocabulary of the house, whether classical, modern, or vernacular, and to influence some of the earliest decisions. Sometimes I use the overall style of the house to guide my design, and at other times I allow contrast to pose an element of surprise. Decisions about architectural details—trim, ceiling treatment, wall finish, column style—significantly shape the character of a space. While a ceiling of coffered plaster introduces a note of grandeur, one of stained wood planking adds warmth and texture, diminishing the scale of a room to create a cozy atmosphere. Drawing attention to the woodwork and moldings by embellishing a room with an intricate cornice or raised paneling fosters formality and a sense of history. Choosing to eliminate trim pieces such as door casings and baseboards injects a fresh, contemporary

look that is edited and sculptural in form. These types of overarching yet precise decisions regarding the direction of a project are best made with input from multiple angles, helping to ensure that the end result is true to the overall vision.

Choices of materials, finishes, and color impact us physically and emotionally in ways that are both obvious and subtle. Cladding the walls, floors, and even cabinets of a room with authentic materials, such as stone cut from a single block, unifies and grounds the design. This effect can also be achieved throughout the house by employing the same wood species in varied treatments—rift-cut, quartersawn, bleached, or cerused—in different rooms. Wood brings warmth, life, and movement to a space. I'm obsessed with showing it in natural form, allowing its grain and character to contribute texture and animation. Metal also has many expressions, whether sleek or burnished with patina, hand-hammered, forged, or sculpted. Each material contributes a compelling tactile finish that enhances its surroundings and reflects light in particular ways. If you repeat a language of certain materials throughout a home, a seamless integrity and clear point of view flows from room to room.

When I travel, I rarely shoot wide-angle photos of rooms or buildings. Instead, I zoom in on the distinct methods in which materials are used and how they intersect and interact with their surroundings. The discoveries I make inspire me to find adventurous ways to work with wood, stone, metal, glass, and fabric. In a recent project, the bathroom was constructed with walls of reeded glass abutting large-format marble tiles, posing a dynamic interplay between gossamer glass and weighty stone. In the dining room of the same home, I fashioned paneling by inlaying walls upholstered in linen with thin metal bands. While the linen absorbed the light and sound, the gleaming brass reflected the candlelight, producing an irresistible space for gathering around the table.

Manipulating scale and circulation also defines the atmosphere of a space. The most interesting homes take you on a journey from compression to release, signaling transitions in experience as you wander through their chambers. A voluminous room invites a feeling of expansiveness, but bigger is not necessarily better. Sometimes exaggerated proportions fail to connect with human scale. Instead of enfolding you, they can make you feel misplaced and lost. This sensation can be alleviated through the right mix of hard and soft finishes and the scale of furnishings. A two-story volume is more accommodating when you add flowing floor-to-ceiling drapery, light fixtures that proportionally complement the scale of the room, and a wall finish that provides textured ambiance. Such gregarious spaces are best paired with the smallest of niches that encompass a place of shelter and intimacy. These are the places where we might gather with friends for close conversation or enjoy hours of reading.

PREVIOUS: A box bay of thin-frame steel windows illuminates a sculptural composition of forms from both back and sides, accentuating the highly textured surfaces of a console table's stone legs. RIGHT: In this dining room, plaster ceiling beams direct the eye upward and outward toward a verdant landscape framed by steel doors. The painterly brush strokes and vivid plum tones of a work on satin by Larissa Lockshin introduce feminine energy to the room's more masculine palette. NEXT: In the study, floor-to-ceiling steel shelving with a backdrop of gray suede sets off the desk's warm walnut grain. Hovering above the room without touching the rift-cut oak paneling, the ceiling floats downward, creating a subtle feeling of compression.

The placement, size, and shape of windows play a vital role in architecture. Natural light may be the single most critical factor influencing how we perceive a room. I often incorporate steel doors and windows into my designs because of the capacity of their slender components to offer unobstructed views and light flow. They are beautiful accents and, based on their design, can transition from the most contemporary of homes to the more traditional. There is also a time and place for the handsome stature of a wooden casement window, the charm of a double-hung one, or subtle statement of a transom. In many instances, a combination of two or more styles is called for. Windows have the potential to become the artwork in a space, as in a master bedroom with little decoration or light that I transformed into an elegant retreat. Simply by flanking the bed with two casement windows crowned by an integrated transom and draping it with delicate linen panels, I was able to produce the formality, symmetry, and layering the room required.

Geographical location rightfully plays a deciding role in architecture. A house in Aspen should look markedly different from one in the Hamptons, inside and out. Questions to consider include what materials best suit the climate and complement the regional architecture. Stone from a local quarry and reclaimed wood salvaged from a nearby barn immediately forge a connection between the house and its surroundings. The placement and size of windows need to respond to weather and locale. In coastal homes, breezy cross-ventilation and cantilevered porches protecting the interior from hot sunlight should be considered. In a house with a dramatic natural setting, large windows strategically oriented to capture views are essential.

You don't need to build from scratch to accomplish a thoughtful, well-executed home. Even in a small renovation, paying attention to architectural detail can significantly distinguish the overall design. I live in a bungalow built in the early 1900s and have enjoyed preserving and reinventing its craftsman details. Originally, there was no ceremonial sense of entry, but now it has a foyer and a central hallway that creates a formal axis of circulation. I included details like transom windows above each door to boost the home's character and pay homage to its heritage. There are so many ways to reinterpret architecture by accentuating or editing existing features, revealing the bones of what's already there, or adding new structure with columns and beams. Salvaged architectural features like floor stones from a French chateau or reclaimed doors heighten character. The range of natural and antique materials available today offers countless means to reawaken each space.

All of these elements, from the site of the building to the trim around the windows, affect your perception of being in a house. Sensing the solidity of materials, finding reassurance in repeated themes, and making discoveries like light from an unseen window that draws you up the stairs are daily moments that shape your life. When architecture and interior design are fully interwoven, the opportunities to mold tangible sensations, as well as indefinable emotions, are infinite. The final effect of a design that thoughtfully marries architecture and interior design is more than just a home. It is an experience you will want to return to, again and again.

Nestled in a wooded glen, this contemporary estate exemplifies a push and pull of modern and traditional elements that reflects the homeowners' diverse tastes and backgrounds. Throughout, old-world finishes like plaster and stained wood juxtapose contemporary appointments. Arranged for relaxed entertaining as well as ample privacy, its design features generously proportioned steel-frame windows and doors to highlight the natural setting. **OPPOSITE**: In the living room, a subtle grid of suede panels and a cast-concrete fire surround wrapping a steel-and-brick firebox forge a dynamic interplay of texture and tone.

ABOVE: Fluted plaster walls and elongated panels of blue wool sateen accentuate the height of the master bedroom and encompass a serene retreat.

ABOVE: Contrast in texture and meticulous detailing defines the living room's architecture, where narrow reveals between ceiling and walls accentuate their character. A plaster surround layered over suede panels adds dimension to the fireplace composition. Layering continues in the arrangement of a gilt-framed mirror over a painting by Mark Fox.

RIGHT: Against the kitchen's inset cabinetry, geometric plaster hood, and polished bluestone flooring, the stove-side drawers and island of reclaimed oak defer to traditional New England style.

OPPOSITE: The ruby color of a vintage Oushak runner introduces another warm, organic element amidst the kitchen's bianco quartzite countertops and white plaster ceiling beams. BELOW: In the dining room, brass-inlaid linen panels and steel windows establish geometric energy balanced by the boat-like form of an enormous cast-glass pendant light. The hand-scraped oak table, velvet-covered chairs, silk-and-wool rug, and brass-and-walnut consoles contribute varied texture and tone.

PREVIOUS: The master suite's his-and-her bathrooms include a strong, masculine chamber clad with dramatically veined Calacatta Lincoln marble. BELOW: Grain-matched walnut and white-lacquered cabinetry frame open-closet space in which a tie rack becomes a colorful work of art. A bubble-like pendant light interjects a touch of levity. OPPOSITE: Her bathroom features chinoiserie-inspired hand-sculpted plaster appliqué depicting graceful limbs of dogwood that produce a delicate dance of light and shadow.

Designed for a family of five who love to entertain and enjoy relaxed time together, this house marries elegance with comfort and durability. With a story rooted in New Orleans, the homeowners desired surroundings that referenced Louisiana Acadian style, achieved through tall French doors, rustic reclaimed beams, and exposed brick accents. Combining the old with the new and the raw with the refined, the interior integrates the rusticity of Creole architecture with a modern sensibility. **OPPOSITE**: The kitchen is richly textured with a sliding barn door of oak, a hand-painted tile backsplash, a sculptural cast-stone hood, and an island topped with slabs of European limestone.

ABOVE: Shiplap walls, wide reclaimed wood floorboards, and brushed oak cabinets give a warm welcome in the family entrance to the house, which serves as both mudroom and kitchen office. The texture of a rustic oak barn door reinforces the historic character of the home.

ABOVE: An arcade of salvaged brick defines separation between the living room and foyer, making a relaxed impression with its warm tone and irregular color and texture. The smooth plaster of the upper walls draws attention to roughly hewn reclaimed beams.

OPPOSITE: In the dining room, the faded paint and aged wood of a trestle table contrast with the silken texture and refined patterning of an Oushak rug. White painted paneling softened by linen-clad walls and linen drapery defines an atmosphere that is simultaneously formal and approachable. **ABOVE:** Tucked into a radiant niche between two stained-oak vanities, the mirrored tub affords a view of the garden through deep-set casement windows. Tumbled limestone tiles introduce subtle pattern.

ABOVE: The front door recalls the purity of Acadian architecture. Hand-plastered walls and simple moldings also pay homage to country French Louisiana style. RIGHT: French doors reclaimed from an Acadian dwelling and a headboard made from an architectural remnant lend historic appeal to the master bedroom's cool blue-and-white palette.

COMPOSITION

Arranging the contents of a space is akin to writing a poem or a symphony. Each word or note is chosen for a reason and curated in a carefully edited way to generate a palpable response. Because the language of architecture and interior design engages so many of the senses—sight, sound, touch, scent—this experience has the potential to be perceived on many levels. When you enter a well-composed room, you may not be able to identify exactly why it makes you feel a certain way, but you know you have been touched and somehow transformed. The arrangement of a room guides the way people use the space, which in turn shapes their state of mind. An effectively orchestrated room has the power to draw you in and reshape the way you live.

The magic of composition has no formula, but it does have framework. There are many things to consider—the overall design, floor plan, flow, and function. I always start with the architecture, referring back to it constantly for decisions about balance and symmetry. Considerations of circulation come next, because the way a home leads you through it is directed by the placement of all its components. Drawing the composition upward, I address every wall, window, and even the ceiling. The colors and materials selected for each room are chosen to complement the overall palette of the house—a consistent vocabulary that should be established at the beginning of the project. It is only at this point that the individual contents of the room—each with its own particular shape, scale, color, and texture—can be placed in a way that harmonize with their surroundings.

One of the challenges of composition is understanding how to arrange countless parts to create a whole that appears both strong and effortless. An equally crucial demand is knowing when to stop. What you don't include is almost more important than what you do. This is what allows the other elements a chance to breathe. Blank space isn't just a place for the eye to rest—it is also a path for the eye to follow. People tend to want to fill every wall, but the purity of nothing creates tranquility. I often strategically utilize white as a room's canvas, then layer it with textures and organically inspired elements. Deep, confident colors like charcoal or saturated gem tones create contrast, focus, and weight in a lightly hued space. When you strike the right balance between the light and dark, the textured and smooth, the things that enliven a room and those that calm it, then nothing distracts and unity is achieved.

For each room, I purposefully decide on a single focal point that will have the greatest emphasis and influence on the rest of the design. In the dining room, it is often the light fixture above the table or a dramatic finish on the walls. In the living room, it might be a seating group, the fireplace, or a work of art. Artwork doesn't always have to take the form of paintings or sculpture. Sometimes the placement of intriguing two-dimensional pieces in a collage or an unexpected wall composition of three-dimensional objects offers artful expression. For a home in Houston, I commissioned an artist who specializes in hand-molded porcelain to craft dozens of disks, each with slightly different forms. Mounted on a wall in a dynamic installation, they instilled a sense of movement to the space that could be appreciated from every perspective.

In kitchens, the central focus is typically the range and vent hood or the island where people are drawn to gather. Delineating the different workspaces of a kitchen with varied materials and finishes leads your eye around the room while offering tactile interest. In the bedroom, the hierarchy usually centers on the bed, where layers of texture can magnify its prominence and evoke a feeling of comfort and luxury. Sometimes the priority of a room is the architecture itself—a barrel-vaulted ceiling that lifts the eye and raises the spirit or a walkway lined with repeating columns that beckons you to explore.

While most clients desire serenity in their homes, there are certain rooms that call for stronger emotions. Contrast can be a subtle yet powerful tool to achieve a more energetic impression. Intense hues and tangible textures combined with more understated surroundings energize a space. I tend toward extremes when it comes to contrast, as in a bathroom design where I paired chiseled-edge stone with brilliantly polished nickel to create an environment that was simultaneously serene and exhilarating. The experience of our surroundings is just as much about what we feel as what we see. Even the smallest moments impact our quality of life. While you may not think about the transition underfoot as you step out of bed onto a velvety silk rug and then to a cool, smooth wood or stone floor, your day is nonetheless enriched.

Juxtaposition is a powerful tool that can be employed to unite disparate parts into engaging compositions. Whether playing with scale, designing the perfect custom piece, or infusing an unexpected pattern or color, it is about unleashing some elements and harnessing others. Placing dissimilar features in close proximity generates tension, and tension is one of the most thrilling things a designer can introduce. Neither bland nor slack, it animates a space and contributes whimsy. That is one reason why I am passionate about combining period pieces with more contemporary styles. Typically, I select a sofa with precise tailoring that acts as a foundation for the room, as well as a staple for comfort. Then I layer in a range of decorative accent chairs and interesting tables to supply character, depth, and charm. When the history and formality of antiques accompany the sleek lines of modern selections, a room assumes inviting livability and the appearance of having been collected over a lifetime.

Visual hierarchy and proportion are especially potent tools for invigorating a room. People can be afraid of dramatic departures in scale, especially when working in tight spaces. However, skillfully wielding the tools of composition can produce a stimulating end result. An enlarged light fixture imbues a space with splendor and awe. An oversize piece of furniture actually allows a smaller space to feel larger. It is imperative to consider what will draw your eye when you enter the room. What will be the loudest player, and what will stay quiet so others can sing? Absorbing the principles of composition, then discovering creative ways to deviate from them, sparks compelling and unpredictable dialogue among elements in a room. All the while, unity and harmony are the end goal. The best compositions have the power to expand awareness and stimulate the soul. The result is a work of art in which to live and breathe.

Upon relocating from New York City to Houston, a family sought a home that celebrated their East Coast-meets-Southern style. Sophisticated contemporary architectural detailing combined with an airy palette and atmosphere of hospitality characterize rooms that are both comfortable and stylish. **PAGE 38**: In the master sitting room, the layering of oak paneling over plaster and a tea-stained painting that floats behind the sofa turns one wall into a three-dimensional composition. **PAGE 41**: The intermittent smooth and chiseled limestone of the fire surround, oak beams, steel-and-wood coffee table, and wool-and-silk rug form a sensuous interplay of natural materials in the living room. **PREVIOUS**: The entrance hall enfolds you in materials and textures that are repeated throughout the home—minimalist oak paneling, luminous limestone pavers, dusky metal, and eye-catching contemporary art. **OPPOSITE**: The tufting of the master bedroom's linen headboard and velvet pillows, cascades of pleated drapery, and slubby carpet furnish a sophisticated retreat.

RIGHT: Strong geometric lines expressed through natural materials impart an atmosphere of graciousness in the living room. Great attention to detail was paid to the integration of hard materials—steel, wood, plaster, and stone—with the lustrous silk rug and velvet pillows contributing necessary softness.

ABOVE LEFT: Neutral-toned rooms circulate around an intensely hued bar where glossy paint and polished-nickel trim express glamour and irresistible appeal. ABOVE RIGHT: In the library, translucent striped-linen drapery filters light, offers privacy, and brings subtle graphic energy to the family room. Soft velvet, lustrous marble, and gleaming brass-and-gilt appointments alternately absorb and reflect the light. OPPOSITE: Within a sleek, modern kitchen, the organic qualities of oak cabinetry, bentwood-and-rattan chairs, and a quartzite backsplash with soft striations integrate the colors and textures of nature.

PREVIOUS: The energetic lines of a portrait by Padaric Kolander and a wall composition of shallow porcelain forms pose a dynamic juxtaposition to the grid-like patterns of the library's oak paneling, bookcases, cast-stone fireplace, and rug. OPPOSITE: The brilliant cobalt tone of a Tony Magar painting infuses intense color into the pearl-like luminosity of a breakfast room flanked by walls of steel and glass. BELOW: Softly finished oak complements the master bathroom's sleek, art deco–inspired components, including vintage travertine floors, charcoal marble counters, and polished nickel-and-glass sconces.

Tucked away in a friendly neighborhood, this serene home was designed for a young family looking for respite from their busy schedules. The clients' favorite shades of whites and pale blush proved ideal for invoking an atmosphere of calm. Within the monotone palette, tactile materials and finishes such as plaster, rift-cut oak, painted brick, and shagreen add variety and increase visual interest. An organizer's dream, the house incorporates floor-to-ceiling cabinetry and hidden storage at every opportunity. **OPPOSITE:** The dark tones of a chair's crushed velvet cushions and bronze frame situated in front of a deeply beveled mantel supply shadowy notes in the white-on-white living room.

ABOVE: A pedestal table of fluted plaster and cube-shaped ottoman reinforce the stair's interplay of straight and curved lines. While complementing the palette, a cowhide rug adds organic shape into the mix.

ABOVE: Bathed by natural light, the fluted barrel ceiling of the living room delivers a calming yet dynamic wave-like impression. Light and shadow are equally important, defining the geometric contours of open shelves and contemporary furnishings.

LEFT: Set off by white trim and furnishings, a pulled-silk wall covering creates a cocoon-like atmosphere in the master bedroom. The silk's irregular striations form a soft backdrop for a dramatic contemporary four-poster bed. A pillow of blush-colored crushed velvet adds a touch of warmth to the cool palette. ABOVE: Hand-painted wallpaper and a pair of brass chandeliers with delicate, branch-like arms establish a dreamy mood in the dining room. Angular appointments including a linear dining table and rectangular plinths dressed with simple plaster bowls bring three-dimensional definition to the space.

OPPOSITE AND ABOVE: The study is clad entirely with gray-washed oak used for paneling with thin, horizontal reveals, minimalist cabinetry, and the vertical fluting of a recessed bookcase. Steel shelves and cabinet hardware and a bronze pendant light bring darker metal tones into the mix, balanced by the bleached oak of the desk, pale silk rug, and translucent drapery.

BELOW: In the butler's pantry, floor-to-ceiling cabinets with shagreen panels and brass trim enclose concealed storage while banks of glass-fronted cabinets provide visual access to their contents. OPPOSITE: In contrast to the crisp, modern lines of the kitchen's slab waterfall island, the curves of a painted-brick, barrel-vaulted ceiling, plaster hood, and veined marble backsplash supply texture and movement.

OPPOSITE: Whispers of gray enter this all-white master bathroom through the veins of the Calacatta Caldia marble on the countertop, floor, and wainscot. Polished nickel reveals in the cabinetry positioned beneath the groin-vaulted plaster ceiling echo the movement of light and shadow. **ABOVE LEFT:** Gently veined marble wainscoting enwraps a bathing bay where linen curtains and roman shades filter light. **ABOVE RIGHT:** In the dressing room, blush-tone verre églomisé panels adorn a bank of cabinet doors and the dressing table, setting up a subtle rhythm with their opaque white surroundings.

CHARACTER

The home is a mirror of the soul, reflecting the spirit of the people who dwell within. As such, it should combine the beliefs and memories they hold dear with the items they cherish most. Entering a home should be an immersive experience saturated by a particular perspective. It is refreshing when someone states his or her point of view honestly and precisely. That same sense of candor can translate to the home. The story of its inhabitants should be instantly apparent, but the surroundings should also suggest that there is more to be learned. When we walk into a well-articulated room, we should feel as though we have been invited into an ongoing conversation. A home with character inspires participation and delivers a lasting impression.

Every home begins as a blank canvas. A fundamental question for interior designers and architects is how to say something truly new and original with the basic building blocks that have existed since the beginning of time. Choices of materials and finishes are one of the most important ways to address this challenge. Authentic, natural materials automatically lend character through tactile experience. Wood may be smooth, rugged, or reclaimed. Stone may be tumbled, honed, or polished. Deliberate variations among materials can set up dynamic interplay, as in a fireplace surround I designed where the limestone shifted from rough, split-face channels to a smooth, honed surface. When light glanced across it, there was a dance of sheen and shadow that accentuated the character and depth of the same material expressed in different form. Some selections mumble, while others dominate the conversation. A discerning designer knows how to ensure that a home's character is reinforced, not overpowered, by these decisions.

One of my roles is to serve as a vessel, taking in my clients' conceptions of beauty and perceptions of a meaningful life in order to deliver surroundings that allow them to live that out. Listening carefully to the way people talk about their homes and the things they value most allows me to discover the roots of their preferences and priorities. I also gain insight by spending time with clients outside of the office. A scouting trip to local art galleries or a stroll through an antique store provides clues about what excites them and what doesn't. When people play an active role in the design of their home, it becomes their personal expression. I enjoy displaying beloved items or reinventing found objects from someone's past in order to forge the sense of individuality that is vital to curating a home with character.

One couple I worked with was deeply inspired by the grandeur and detail of a particular church ceiling. By using reclaimed materials to adapt the design for the ceiling of their living room, we were able to recall its magnificence. Surrounded by walls of antique stone from France, the room possessed qualities of weight, depth, and patina. This same couple had gathered a collection of antique Persian rugs woven in rich gem tones. My first instinct was to shy away from their bold dyes and patterns because I feared they might distract from the room's already strong forms and textures. Instead, I allowed my clients' passion to lead the way, using the vivid hues of the rugs to guide the palette of the room while offsetting them with neutral shades. Ultimately, the power of the stone and wood balanced the impact of the rugs, melding them into a design that was harmonious and uniquely relevant to the people who live there.

Sometimes clients are captivated by a certain time or place and want their home to recapture what they love most about it. For a couple with an affinity for Louisiana's early Acadian architecture, I designed rooms featuring exposed vintage brick accented by antiques from New Orleans. The ambiance and age of these ingredients called forth the atmosphere of the location and period that resonated deeply for them, allowing them to revisit a special memory every time they came home.

Instilling character in a home is a voyage of adventure that helps us learn what matters most and awakens us to the nuances of design. When my clients walk into their finished homes, my hope is that they will immediately recognize themselves in it. The character of a house comes from the heart of the inhabitants. A fusion of personal psyches, experiences, and rituals, the home is a sacred place. It is the cocoon where we are revived and comforted and the haven into which we invite people to feel the same way. This is where we hold our treasure—both material and spiritual. It is where the divine whispers amidst the daily noise, revealing a highly individual vision of the well-lived life.

Shaded by mature oak trees, this Tudor-style home was fully re-imagined and restored for modern comfort and a mood of history and romance. Furnishings ranging from the simple to the elegant, distinctive lighting, and tailored upholstery allow the clients' collection of antique rugs to become focal points in many of the rooms. **OPPOSITE:** Richly burnished industrial copper lighting illuminates the breakfast room. Windows with frames set deeply into the walls give the impression of antique leaded glass.

ABOVE AND RIGHT: A hammered-copper farmhouse sink and hand-carved limestone hood bring artisanship to this kitchen. Although a muted color story, it is deepened by varied materials and finishes including reclaimed oak flooring, glazed backsplash tiles, and etched-glass globe pendants. The darkly painted wood of the doors and windows creates an intentional framework for enticing views of the surrounding landscape.

OPPOSITE: In the master sitting area, painted walls, linen drapery, a limestone table, and caned sofa express shades of ivory that allow the intense hues of the bedroom rug to take center stage. ABOVE LEFT: The high, vaulted ceiling of the bedroom creates a lofty effect that is mitigated by warm tones of reclaimed planks. Placed near the bed, a writing table performs double duty as desk and nightstand. ABOVE RIGHT: The gold-and-rust veins of onyx employed for the wet bar's backsplash, shelf, and countertop heighten the burnished grain of walnut cabinetry.

BELOW: With rugged carving and heavy bronze knobs, deeply grained doors of reclaimed oak form a dramatic contrast with the master bathroom's pale, inlaid-marble floor and white walls. OPPOSITE: Heavy oak beams arranged in an X-shaped composition become the focal point of the dining room. A large iron chandelier hanging from the intersection of the beams brings the height of the dramatic ceiling down to human scale. Leather-wrapped wingback chairs complement the generous proportions of the room. NEXT: Painted shiplap covers the bathroom's ceiling, accentuating its complex lines and reflecting light from expansive windows. Marble surfaces, gold-toned fixtures, richly grained walnut, and an Oushak rug bring color and luster to the room, and the glass-walled shower injects a contemporary touch.

The interior of this Victorian home in Colorado was refashioned in contemporary style with a focus on large windows that frame dramatic mountain views. With the exception of a media room enveloped in deep shades of blue, all the walls, trim, and ceilings are painted the same shade of white. This monochromatic environment provides an ideal setting for the clients' museum-worthy collection of contemporary art. **OPPOSITE:** The living room's black marble mantelpiece complements the graphic triptych of drawings by Robert Rauschenberg. Curves reign supreme in furnishings that include a serpentine sofa, oval travertine coffee table, and bent-wood chairs upholstered in a stand-out shade of blue.

ABOVE: The arc of the sofa offsets the angularity of the living room's architecture, which features an ebony-stained wet bar embellished by a marble backsplash with strongly diagonal veining.

ABOVE: With walls lacquered indigo blue and a ceiling to match, the media room possesses an inviting feeling of compression that balances the lofty proportions of nearby rooms. Within the dark setting, a colorful op-art painting by Robert Swain becomes a luminous highlight.

OPPOSITE: In the breakfast room, a slab of marble with dynamic veins stretching to the upper limits of the space becomes a work of art, producing an effect that is simultaneously lively and serene. Beneath a white pendant light, the plum-colored linen upholstery of midcentury modern chairs injects tonal contrast. ABOVE: In the adjacent kitchen, the same marble is employed to clad the countertop, hood, and walls against which a wooden shelf appears to levitate. On the opposing wall, white floor-to-ceiling cabinetry creates a sleek foil for the marble's organic patterning.

LEFT: The daughter's bedroom is imbued with a soft, pretty palette drawn from the painterly floral pattern of linen drapery pocketed into dentil crown molding. A host of painted-brass butterflies hover against one wall, creating an ethereal aura anchored by the bed's tufted-velvet headboard. ABOVE: A work on paper by Agnes Martin perches on a ledge of white wainscoting near a midcentury modern lounge chair.

ABOVE: Layering plays a dramatic role in the powder room, where a fluted walnut cabinet with a marble top and metal vessel sink projects from a wall of matte black tile. An antique mirror framed in glistening brass floats above it, reflecting a graphic black-and-white globe pendant light.

ABOVE: Following the roofline of a second-story gable, a slanted ceiling descends to form a cozy nook for lounging on a vintage leather sofa. A variety of textures including leather, chrome, acrylic, and the raised pile of a wool rug add dimension to the room's pared-down palette.

ABOVE LEFT: In a master sitting room featuring works by Agnes Martin and Richard Serra, midcentury modern chairs in smoke-colored velvet and a hair-on-hide ottoman present appealing tactile surfaces. **ABOVE RIGHT:** Exposed brass plumbing is mounted directly to the glass wall of the master bathroom's shower. **OPPOSITE:** Marble wainscoting brings organic pattern into play, contrasting with the linear raw-oak and unlacquered brass vanity. More graphic energy comes through a floor striped with contrasting types of marble. Light entering through a deep gabled window accentuates the geometric forms of the room.

PALETTE

When commencing a work of art, an artist arranges dabs of paint on a palette that will soon be scraped and mixed together. As the separate colors are mingled and applied to the canvas with intentional brushstrokes, they begin to form a composition that reflects the artist's original conception. A painter may not use exactly the same pigments or brushwork in every painting, but there is a consistency that marks it as the work of a certain artist, painted from a chosen palette. The interior designer's palette is comprised of color, texture, pattern, and patina—ingredients that are combined through my own work in a recognizable aesthetic that is neither traditional nor modern, but timeless and curated. Each home shares the common threads of elegance and refinement, interwoven with approachability and livability.

Color is the design factor that most obviously affects our moods and the ambiance of a room. I begin each project by devising a universal color palette or story, then play off it throughout the different spaces of the home. Infusing designs with nature's colors brings the outdoors in and puts our spirits instinctively at ease. Nature's spectrum is infinite, spanning the saturated neutrals of wheat and stony gray; nuanced shades such as chalky blue, olive green, and rusty orange; and gem tones—dark sapphire blues, emerald greens, and deep amethyst purples.

When subtle colors are used as the foundation for a room, more intense hues can be introduced as accents through fabrics, furniture, rugs, and artwork. Even robust colors like auburn and turquoise can translate into serene settings when they are incorporated holistically, permeating a room from its wall finishes to the furnishings. Then, they translate into an almost neutral canvas against which contrast, texture, and form can influence the design and singular decorative selections can become major protagonists. In a mountain home where white was the dominant color, I swathed the den in an unexpectedly intense indigo blue, layering shades of the color throughout the room in various textures, from the shiny lacquered walls and matte velvet sofa to the silk trim adorning the roman shades. Within this monotone context, an abstract painting by color theorist Robert Swain asserted a clear and dynamic statement.

Texture is a prerequisite for a substantive, well-executed palette. It makes a space feel warm and enticing, drawing us in and inviting us to touch, feel, and fully experience our surroundings. Without it, a neutral interior will appear like a flat sea of beige. Contrast through texture brings a space to life, especially when it comes through nature's own textiles of long-hair hide, soft suede, and pebbly shagreen. I recently used shagreen to inlay the cabinetry of a butler's pantry, outlining it with a thin brass channel to add the ultimate touch of luxury. In a guest bedroom, I experimented with the nuanced characters of different woven fabrics, combining an antiqued-velvet headboard with a gauzy linen canopy. The way light acted differently on their surfaces—sinking into the matte weave of the linen and lingering on the velvet, illuminating its intentional imperfections—was stunning.

When I travel in Europe, I pay attention to the material and trim of antique drapery made from handcrafted lace, embossed textiles, and silk brocade embellished with gold and silver threads. Inspired by this old-world beauty, I extract its essence into contemporary expression, using modern-day textiles embroidered with metal threads or interwoven with raw, natural fibers to convey the same lavish sensory experience. In fresh takes on classic themes, I have fashioned full, billowing drapery from jacquard or wool and used simple, sheer curtains of linen *voile*, French for veil, in main living spaces. When translucent or highly embellished fabrics are paired with the organic qualities of materials in their natural form—veined marble, petrified wood, woven sea grass, alabaster—the effect is dramatic.

While the tactile properties of texture center us in the present moment, patina links us with the past by offering tangible evidence of time's passage. I think of patina as a living finish because the surfaces of certain materials change constantly in response to the effects of time, the elements, and the touch of the human hand. Consider, for example, solid brass lavatory fixtures with levers whose contours are polished to a shine by daily use while the crevices acquire deep brown and green patina.

PREVIOUS: In the master bedroom, smooth plaster walls create a backdrop for a wall sculpture by Donald Martiny in blush tones—a soft but striking complement to the gray-green velvet headboard. The floral forms of a plaster-coated chandelier visually lightens the weight of the ceiling beams. RIGHT: The organic textures of framed herbieres, shagreen and brass nightstands, alabaster lamps, and a natural jute rug bring tactile interest to the all-white guest room. NEXT: While the ashlar stone wall, heavy oak beams, and sturdy trestle table establish an impression of solidity, the dining room's steel-and-glass walls release the space into a horizon of sea and sky. The hues of the waterscape inspired the blue, gray, and white palette of the room.

Or picture an oft-turned brass doorknob which, never lacquered, gleams dusky gold. Marble counters inevitably stain, scratch, and acquire indentations with wear. To me, these imperfections equate to beauty, calling to mind the surfaces of centuries-old buildings in Italy. Often, I will order objects months before they are installed so we can leave them exposed in order to tarnish and age. Not everyone has the courage and patience to live with finishes that evolve over time, remaining perpetually "imperfect", but patina can burnish a home's palette and identify it as a place for living, not just for show.

Pattern possesses the inherent ability to animate spaces. Wallpaper and fabrics are the most obvious ways to inject pattern, whether energetic or orderly. Herringbone, which reminds me of men's bespoke suiting, is one of my preferred choices for upholstery. I am also drawn to the edited lines of stripes and small-scale geometric patterns, as well as the softer forms of color-blocked designs. Pattern can be expressed monochromatically through weave and pile, as with nubby bouclé, quilted fabrics, and matelassé. It can also be incorporated through drapery, like the chinoiserie-inspired floral motif I chose to establish the color palette for an entire room. Global accents like a kilim rug or piece of antique Kuba cloth framed and mounted on a wall can become the artwork in an otherwise serene room. There is also a time and place for letting pattern become the overall statement. In a small study I designed, the most prominent feature was a sofa upholstered in a geometric motif in shades of black, blush, and dark green. Once the walls were painted the same green, the sofa became the strongest player in the room while still meshing with its surroundings.

Nearly every material has the potential to be formed into pattern, whether fluted plaster, reeded glass, etched metal, carved stone, or wood parquet. Manipulating the natural essence of a material in a way that makes it more compelling is one way I love to employ pattern. Rather than install traditional tile in a bathroom, I fashioned stripes by alternating slabs of distinctly veined marble with thin strips of unlacquered brass. When inlaid wood flooring is intricately arranged and stained in different tones, or recessed portions of paneling are dressed with a decorative wall covering, the repeating shapes convey rhythm to their environment.

I am always looking for opportunities to push the boundaries of my palette, imagining innovative ways to forge alluring and arresting relationships among materials. But no matter how expertly a designer uses color, texture, patina, and pattern, the three-dimensional result will fall flat unless meaning—which I consider the fourth dimension—is engaged. It is important never to overshadow the personality of the clients nor to neglect the possessions they prize most. At the end of an installation, I carefully position these items in places of honor. I have showcased a jewelry box that belonged to a client's grandmother as the sole accessory in her dressing room and displayed a cherished collection of antique copper pots on a dramatic rack above a kitchen window. When treated with the same respect and tenderness their owners feel for them, these objects can become the favorite features in a room. As people grow and change and their lifestyles shift, the best palettes provide an enduring, understated foundation for their lives and the things they hold dear.

Floating on the shores of a lake, this peaceful Texas Hill Country home is a gathering place for three generations of a tightly-knit family. Integrated throughout, white Austin limestone harmonizes the home with its surroundings. Sleek steel doors and windows offset by ruggedly solid walls of Vermeer-cut limestone frame unobstructed views of the lake. **OPPOSITE:** In the kitchen, solid stone walls with saw marks provide textural contrast to shiny countertops. Antique meets modern in the juxtaposition of the deeply incised grain of the sliding pantry door and smoother rift-cut oak cabinetry and shelving.

PREVIOUS: Honey-toned, hand-hewn wood beams warm the kitchen's light palette, as do brass-trimmed seeded-glass pendant lights. While the veins of the countertops echo the finish of rift-cut cabinetry and cast bronze hardware, the simplicity of the plaster hood provides a place for the eye to rest. OPPOSITE: In the dining room, ripples of soft blue linen upholstery mediate the precise form of the plaster table, and wood beams and limestone paving balance the geometry of the pendant light and windowpanes. ABOVE LEFT: In the outdoor kitchen, a sleek plaster hood floats against patterned encaustic tiles incorporated into a smeared-mortar stone wall. ABOVE RIGHT: Plaster arches form a series of vestibules along a grand hallway.

ABOVE: The powder room's tawny rift-cut oak paneling and onyx countertop present a shift in tone from its plaster surroundings. The integration of gray limestone into the buff-colored stone floor used throughout the house also signals a change in mood. RIGHT: A beveled, cast-stone mantel juxtaposes crisp lines against the rugged limestone wall. Fashioned from the same reclaimed oak as the ceiling beams, a chunky coffee table blends with its surroundings.

OPPOSITE: Framed French letters illuminated with colorful accents echo the surrounding tones of a blush velvet pillow, blue linen cushion, linen roman shades, and cut-pile silk rug. ABOVE: A tall, arched window, oak ceiling beams, and the mirrors' beveled plaster surround contribute architectural dimension to the master bath. Fluted vanities, hexagonal marble floors, and a voluminous tub integrate texture through their varied surfaces.

Graced with stunning waterfront views, this remodeled bayside retreat simplifies daily living and makes for effortless entertaining. Structural changes were made to the layout and excess architectural details removed. Textiles that breathe and feel cool to the touch, such as linen and cotton, were chosen, alongside high-performance materials selected to withstand the demands of a hot and humid climate. **OPPOSITE:** An atmosphere of serenity pervades the master suite where layers of diaphanous curtains and woven roman shades frame views while also offering respite from the coastal light. A sculptural piece of driftwood makes a strong yet subtle statement above the two-tone, four-poster bed with a glazed linen headboard. The strié carpet placed atop the bleached wood floor adds softness underfoot.

ABOVE: Unadorned windows deliver expansive views of the water in the dining area, which features a streamlined wooden table surrounded by darker leather-backed chairs. An elongated onyx bowl serves as a centerpiece uniting the room's palette of neutrals.

ABOVE: Encompassing the living, dining, and kitchen areas, the great room is centered around a minimalist concrete fireplace with a rustic, oak-beam mantel. A rattan armchair and hair-on-hide ottomans are handsome accents that can be easily relocated to accommodate conversation.

LEFT: White shiplap with touches of misty blue and sea green form a restful palette for the master bedroom. On the far side of the bed, a simple wood desk serves as a nightstand—a place for productivity amidst relaxed surroundings. ABOVE: In the adjacent master sitting room, also a bedroom for visiting grandchildren, a wooden drum pendant and rope storage ottomans soften the straight lines of the bookcases and striped rug. A seascape photograph by Bob Tabor reflects the ocean waves outside the windows.

BELOW AND OPPOSITE: There is deceptive simplicity to the master bathroom, which features an elegant tub surround and matching countertops. The same material frames a pair of mirrors on which silver sconces appear to float above a weightier walnut vanity. Shiplap walls, woven wood roman shades, and smoky floor tiles lend casual textures that offset the formality of surrounding finishes.

ILLUMINATION

Nothing else possesses the transformative power of light. It is essential for life and growth. It empowers our vision, informs the way we experience our surroundings, and influences the way we feel. Light transfigures every material it touches, presenting the world to us by creating color and revealing texture. Every shade and surface responds to it uniquely and each form finds expression in its presence. Light renders life to all the elements within a room, knitting them together into an environment that affects us on every level. It has the power to completely shift the function, ambiance, and mood of any space. It may be the most fundamental element to consider in design.

Adding natural light is the best thing you can do for a room—it brings a beauty that is incomparable. That is why windows are my idea of the ultimate luxury. As daylight passes through them, traveling across a room and touching its contents, its minute-by-minute progression is a form of theater. When you understand how to capture natural light and manipulate it to enhance a room's appearance and function, you are able to influence the experience of being there. For this endeavor, window coverings are essential, performing double duty as a functional necessity and a decorative flourish. I try never to block windows with drapery, instead I celebrate them and allow for their maximum impact. In most main living spaces, I prefer sheers for their airy softness and gentle way they veil light and views. In bedrooms, lavish folds of blackout drapery layered with sheers are the ideal choice for heightening the glamour of the space while also controlling light and providing privacy. I often mix in roman shades made from natural woven fibers for their rich texture, whether solo or in tandem with drapery.

Without an intentional lighting plan, even the best-designed space feels unfinished and flat. When illumination is poor, a sense of claustrophobia and dullness sets in. Layering light shapes the character of a room, whether as an oasis of serenity or a space filled with drama. Drapery, window shades, adjustable controls, indirect-, task-, and accent lighting offer many ways to harness and focus light. Finding the proper balance of ambient and task lighting for each room is an art in and of itself. Overall lighting that brightens a room and its functions is the foundational element, but peppering the ceiling with recessed fixtures that oversaturate a space with one-dimensional light is to be avoided. Combining natural and overhead illumination with spots, floor lamps, and table lamps, defining pools of light, and emphasizing shadows showcases the most notable features in the room. Art lighting is a necessity for accentuating the forms of sculpture and unique beauty of paintings. Mirrors, art objects in their own right, reflect and magnify light and animate walls.

Light fixtures are not meant to serve solely as a source of illumination. While functionality is key, they can also become focal points and even a room's standout feature. I often employ them as a sculptural presence that may only emit a hint of light. Instead of using two chandeliers in a living room with multiple seating areas, I custom-designed a single, long, meandering chandelier with sparkling glass shades that contributed dynamic interest overhead. Surprising scale and form can turn a fixture into an unforgettable statement, as with an immense iron chandelier with dozens of slender, upswept arms fashioned to hang from the center of a voluminous living room.

The orientation of rooms is a factor that often goes unconsidered. When I can allow gentle northern light to suffuse a room, I will. Rooms with northern exposures are permeated with soft, indirect light that promotes a calming atmosphere throughout the day. In these rooms, windows can be left uncovered or curtained with sheers, without worry of harsh light or sun damage. With other exposures, direct light may stream in during mornings or afternoons, creating striking shadows and dynamic movement. Sheers that diffuse light, blinds that control it, and lined curtains that obscure it offer artful ways to manage and transform its intensity, which, though stunning, can be overpowering at times.

Proper illumination is not simply about adding and controlling light. It is also about knowing when to embrace shadow. This is an art that invites us to consider the different properties of luminosity and darkness, to celebrate their extremes, and invite them to intermesh. A complex interplay of light and shadow enhances our awareness of the nuances of color, whether strong, deep tones or delicate ones, and of texture, both subtle and bold. If lighting is insufficient or harsh, it destroys our perception of color and dimension and undermines our mood. We should never lose sight of the fact that light is meaningful to the spirit and has the power to enrich the quality of our lives.

With a focus on time-honored materials including leaded glass, reclaimed wood, and antique fixtures, this new home feels anything but new. A classic color palette of French blues, whites, burgundy, and charcoal meld into a warm and inviting environment for a young family of six. Fostering the clients' love for entertaining, the house is replete with plentiful spaces for gatherings ranging from sophisticated dinners to children's slumber parties. **OPPOSITE:** Even when the lights are off, the pendant lamp of aged-brass strips forms a powerful presence in the study. Natural light accentuates the grain of wood paneling and patterned textiles. Bronze-and-brass sconces inset in a niche add an element of task lighting, brightening the colors of an oil landscape by G. Harvey mounted on a dark green moleskin panel.

ABOVE: A uniform shade of gray unites a bank of windows in the dining room, transforming them into a wall of light. The oak ceiling glows at night when uplit by an iron-and-wood chandelier and the concrete table forms a white highlight in the room's center.

ABOVE: In the kitchen, the reclaimed oak flooring, planked ceiling treatment, and blue ceramic backsplash unite with the materials and colors of the adjacent dining room. An island of fluted oak, cast-bronze light fixtures, and leaded-glass door panel reference traditional material and craft.

PREVIOUS: The open floor plan allows each room to reflect a consistent, luminous palette as seen in the sheen of antiqued velvet upholstery, leather ottomans, and a gilt-wood chair. OPPOSITE: In the master bedroom, linen drapery, rust-colored velvet, and a saturated Oushak rug absorb light and sound. The gilded antique mirror and French silver-leaf chandelier provide dazzling counterpoint. ABOVE LEFT: Fixtures chosen for their light-enhancing qualities, including a translucent onyx lamp and sconces gilded in twenty-two karat gold, illuminate the cathedral ceiling. ABOVE RIGHT: With no natural light, the master dressing room benefits from strategically placed directional lights that function like art lighting to emphasize the rich grain of the two-toned wood and painted cabinetry.

ABOVE: In the master bathroom, leaded glass windows shine light onto the highly reflective polished nickel plumbing fixtures of a freestanding tub. RIGHT: A beaded-crystal chandelier, mirrored medicine cabinets, and hammered-silver sconces add sparkle to an ethereal palette defined by floral drapery, marble flooring, and Calacatta countertops.

This master suite renovation presented particular challenges due to the compartmentalized floor plan and lack of natural light. Increasing and optimizing the amount of light available to the bathroom and connected dressing closet became the project's primary focus. A variety of solutions were employed, including devising innovative ways to capture and enhance natural light, combining different types of artificial illumination, and harnessing the reflective properties of natural materials. The end result is a suite of rooms that range from the brightly illuminated bathroom and a glowing dressing room wrapped in wood to a master bedroom decorated in handsome masculine tones. **OPPOSITE:** Newly constructed skylight panels inspired by Mediterranean solariums brighten the entire bathroom. Sunlight from a trio of large windows cut into an exterior wall spills beyond the shower into the main vanity areas. A handsome pendant anchors the new layout above the tub, while the clouds and sea of a Dutch maritime scene echo the veins of the surrounding marble slabs.

OPPOSITE: Walls of honed Calacatta marble were carved into wainscoting and paneling patterns, precisely planned to frame plumbing and lighting fixtures. Brass inlays the floating walnut vanity, trims mirrors inset into the marble slab, and appears in sleek art deco–inspired sconces. **ABOVE:** Combining wood with unlacquered brass, the plumbing fixtures reflect the master suite's material palette in miniature scale.

OPPOSITE: Illuminated by large windows, the marble-clad shower room's walls and ceiling become light-amplifying surfaces. On either end of the space, frosted glass-and-metal cabinets hold toiletries and towels. BELOW: With light emanating from an overhead pendant, a pair of sconces, and LEDs integrated into the millwork, the dressing room has no need of natural illumination. Opulent finishes including oak wall paneling, leather drawer pulls, a generously scaled dressing table, and leather bench showcase the clothing as if in a luxury bespoke clothier.

ABOVE: Outlined in crisp white trim, the master bedroom's black walls and drapery establish an energizing rhythm of light and dark. Bathed in natural light, spooled-wood chairs with off-white cushions flank a beige camelback sofa appointed by a pair of ottomans with quilted white leather sides. OPPOSITE: The masculine tones of the master bedroom provide handsome contrast to the bright, white bathroom. Nestled inside a canopy of black-and-white drapery panels, the winged-leather headboard and layered bedding furnish an inviting retreat for rest and rejuvenation.

DETAIL

Our lives are made up of innumerable moments that unfold over time and hold meaning for us. My calling is to capture and transmit the power of these fleeting instances into enduring, dimensional reality that reveals the sacred in the everyday. Details are the magic in a room—enchanting hints that pique our interest, attract closer inspection, and invite exploration. Sometimes they are so subtle that we can't quite pinpoint what it is that draws our attention or triggers a certain memory or state of mind. Small, well-considered gestures like the hand-carved fluting down the leg of a console or a seat cushion's finely crafted trim speak quietly, but still make their presence known. When we pause in our busy day and allow these finer points to focus our attention on our surroundings for even a few seconds, they have the power to engage us in a very particular here and now.

Details offer opportunities for invention, playfulness, complexity, and depth. An astute layering of the smaller possessions is critical to making a home complete. At its best, interior design is a delicate dance that sways back and forth between consideration of the whole and preoccupation with the smallest part. My home is a test laboratory where I am forever deconstructing rooms and reinventing them by incorporating new things and recasting existing ones in fresh compositions. My favorite paintings travel from room to room. Items I collect on my walk through life find places of honor on tabletops and shelves. I particularly relish the challenge of using found objects that some might consider plain or even unattractive in unforeseen ways, giving them new meaning and beauty. Creatively reinterpreted, a peculiar stone found on a mountain hike or a

weathered piece of driftwood can become a talisman that sparks memories of a special time and the ones with whom you shared it.

Each home should be filled with treasures whose value is uniquely understood by its inhabitants. Even though others may not recognize the significance of these things, they still enrich their experience of being there. When designing a dining room for a family whose members included children adopted from other parts of the world, I found a way to tell their story on the walls through custom illustrations of birds from the countries where each child was born. These were integrated into a hand-painted chinoiserie-inspired mural that illustrated in quite a literal way that everyone should have a seat at the table. In another dining room, I allowed my clients' collection of hundreds of Scotch bottles to be the main focal point, becoming a work of art that served both as homage to the husband's ancestry and a souvenir of the couple's countless voyages to the country. Displayed in cased shelves with inset lighting, these objects offer a glittering indulgence for the eye as well as cues for recounting the stories behind them.

Details should feel effortless, never studied nor contrived—but seemingly insouciant details actually take a lot of time to execute correctly. When I design a custom piece of furniture or light fixture, I calculate the precise ways in which the materials will come together. How will a leather welt fasten the linen upholstery of a stool to the wooden base? At what point will the reeded glass shade of a pendant light meet the antique brass frame? The authenticity and depth of each object's materials endow it with

beauty, but it is the thought devoted to seemingly minor decisions, right down to the exact screws used in a fastening, that completes its elegance and grace. Although minute, such details still possess the capacity to enrich.

Nothing compares with fine craftsmanship for its power to bring an object or an entire design to life. It conveys the touch and imagination of the particular artisans who have brought their unique talent and vision to expression. I find it a great gift to collaborate with skilled masters who realize my imaginings through their craft, sometimes even more exquisitely than I could have envisioned. When I commissioned a carpenter to hand-plane paneled doors of rift-cut oak that would be appointed by cast-bronze door hardware, I knew they would become jewels in the house. But it was not until I experienced the barely perceptible irregularities of the planed wood surface, the movement of the grain, and the weight of the heavy bronze door handles that I fully perceived what character they contributed.

When I visit historic homes and buildings, I often find myself noticing subtle elements that might escape other's attention: the leg of a chair, the casing on a doorway, or a pool of shadow cast by lamplight in the corner of a room. I enjoy combing through photos from my trips, rediscovering something I've seen before and allowing it to inform what I am working on now. I often gain inspiration from the past, finding ways to simplify traditional forms for a more up-to-date result. While there are countless opportunities to reinterpret bygone details in modern ways, moldings and trim are among my favorites. Decorative details such as a lavish

fringe, a pleated skirt, or reeded molding can add a dose of needed historical charm and warmth to a contemporary interior.

Sometimes we become complacent and even disillusioned in our homes, allowing treasured possessions to fade into the background or entirely losing our ability to see them. Yet, when we celebrate the things we own in unexpected ways, we can reinvent them, propelling them to the forefront again. As years pass and our lifestyles and interests change, new objects will always be introduced, but we must not forget the simple truth that moving the treasures we already possess can refresh them and transform our homes. It's astonishing but true—changing the styling of a space completely modifies the entire sensory experience of being there. This is something guests have an acute ability to notice, sensing that things have shifted, however so slightly, since their previous visit.

There is a final tier of personal attention and graciousness that enhances the allure of the home and makes guests feel cherished. Glowing candles, the softest throw strewn across the foot of a well-made bed—these thoughtful gestures shape the emotional character of a space. Something as simple as freshly cut flowers or greenery contribute a living connection with nature. Clients often ask me for a list of the flowers I've placed for them so they can recreate the arrangements, but I encourage them to try other varieties at different seasons, exploring what new scents and colors will bring to the space. When the design of a room is permitted to evolve, whether day by day or year by year, it becomes a living, breathing embodiment of our life and history.

PAGE 138: Vertical lines of rift-cut white oak paneling intersect dark walnut cabinetry with steel framing and gray suede doors. PAGE 141: Elongated marble tiles, a wall-mounted faucet, and tightly fitted mirror make the most of the slender space between a window and storage towers in this master bathroom. PREVIOUS: Shades of green play off one another in a niche lined with dark velvet enclosing a G. Harvey landscape and Hahn Dynasty–style vase. OPPOSITE: Matte black fixtures amplify the graphic energy of this powder room's striking mural wallpaper. ABOVE LEFT: In this California breakfast room, hand-painted wallpaper portrays wind-blown leaves. Hummingbirds, one for each member of the family, are depicted amongst the foliage. ABOVE RIGHT: In the adjoining kitchen, an ever-changing collection of vintage artwork and earthenware dishes resides on a marble ledge.

PREVIOUS: Custom-cut tiles of marble form this master bathroom's walls, countertops, and floors. Two mirrors set into the marble wall flank a brass-trimmed cabinet with milk-glass panels. **ABOVE LEFT**: In a dining room, a hand-painted chinoiserie mural depicts flora and fauna that includes birds symbolizing different members of the family who share this home. **ABOVE RIGHT**: Brass escutcheons add sheen at the base of hand-hammered iron balusters, enhancing the drama and elegance of a staircase.

ABOVE: In this powder room, hand-painted tile provides a graceful backdrop for a roughly textured plaster sink and etched mirror, proving that bold pattern and varied materials make for a memorable impression.

ABOVE LEFT: Hinged walnut panels enfold the bed and nightstands in a master bedroom. Against the dark wood, brass-and-gilt trim and a contemporary alabaster lamp make subtle statements. ABOVE RIGHT: Oak trim wraps the recessed face of a cast-stone fireplace, balancing the warmth of wood with the cool, sculptural quality of stone. OPPOSITE: Fluted oak cabinets with marble countertops, matte plaster walls, and highly reflective antique-mirror sconces each react differently in the master bathroom's plentiful light.

OPPOSITE: The plaster interiors of bookcases flanking a reeded fire surround are tinted in varying shades of white and gray. Blond oak shelves inlaid with brass promote luxurious minimalism. **ABOVE:** Painted paneling integrated into the staircase accentuates the dynamic thrust of the steps. A dark iron railing and a runner anchored by corresponding stretcher bars trace this diagonal movement.

BELOW: In the master sitting room, the rhythmic lines of fluted plaster walls create a modern backdrop for a contemporary suede lounge chair and iron side table. OPPOSITE: Attention to detail is particularly important in an all-white space like this bedroom, which is appointed with touches of gleaming brass, a textural raised-pile rug, and mercury-glass bell-jar lantern. NEXT: Photographs taken by the homeowner's friend claim special spots in the living room and bedroom of this guest apartment. Organic textures, contoured furnishings, and a neutral color story speak quietly in unison.

ABOVE: Painted paneling trimmed with curved corbels encase the tub of this master bathroom in an intimate niche. An antique mirror and carefully placed accessories soften and warm the palette.

ABOVE: Balancing the ornate with the simple, the precise lines of a velvet headboard function as a base note for the rococo flourishes of a petite gilded mirror and intricate bedside tables.

OPPOSITE: Small spaces deserve imaginative details like the highly patterned fabric covering this office's walls and sconces. The built-in desk, matching trim, and a muted painting by Mallory Page allow the eye to rest within the sea of pattern. ABOVE: Bars, like powder rooms, call for beautifully executed details such as gleaming knobs, metal mesh, a charming faucet, and artful adornments.

SIMPLICITY

Cultivating soulful simplicity is a complex endeavor that requires recognizing what is crucial and editing out the rest. The idea of simplicity is counterintuitive in our culture—it is not usually our first inclination to hold back or subtract. But it is important to learn how to peel away the unnecessary. When we strip down to the essential, we arrive at a point of purity, of knowing what matters and what is most significant. In the words of Socrates, "The secret to happiness is not found in seeking more, but in developing the capacity to enjoy less." The same is true of interior design. Its aim is to say more with less, allowing the fundamental elements to speak articulately. Editing may be the most difficult task to master, but when done well, it is transformational.

Simplicity is the art of creating order and beauty by skillfully assembling the many ingredients of design. It provides an invisible yet perceptible foundation for discovering what is meaningful and important to the whole. I am mindful of it throughout the entire design process, always asking what might need to be left out and what might need to be added. Simplicity is not about minimalism—it's about finding the right balance to shape the experience you desire. Composition, material, craftsmanship, palette, and lighting all come into play, married in a manner that reflects the homeowners' personalities and what they need in each particular place.

Negative space is just as important as decorated space. Every room requires a moment of pause. Using sophisticated variations of white or even an entirely unadorned wall allows a room to breathe. As in fashion, it's better not to cover a house from head to toe. Coco Chanel offered enduring wisdom when she said, "Before you leave the house, look in the mirror and take one thing off." A room that deftly embraces negative space never feels incomplete—rather, it bestows welcomed opportunities for the eye to rest. There is great liberation in giving ourselves wide enough margin to truly relish and partake of our surroundings. A little negative space also affords the capacity to receive the clients' stories. A good designer will refrain from "over-designing" in order to allow clients to grow into their homes over time, placing prized possessions and adding evidence of their ongoing lives.

Never underestimate the force and silence of white when working toward simplicity. White has many properties. It builds anticipation of what the eye will encounter next and manifests colors and textures in ways that are undiluted and bold. Several years ago, I spent some time volunteering at a homeless shelter in New York City. When I commented on the almost monastically simple interiors—all white walls, historic stained-wood floors, simplified textures and decor—the caretaker explained that the intent was to create a peaceful retreat from the turmoil of the streets, where the people they served could quiet their lives and focus on healing. I will always remember that lesson. Don't we all need a place to escape and allow the beauty of home to revive and heal us? To discover where we find relief is to find where we belong.

A trace of simplicity can be found in great interiors of many styles, even the most highly ornamented. Reinterpreting their essence involves finding the root form that lies within and honoring it. This practice makes it possible to take something complex and enhance its beauty through clarity. When I was asked to bring a midcentury modern aesthetic to a Victorian house in Telluride, Colorado, that possessed all the architectural embellishments of the period, I turned first to white. By adding appropriate moldings, opening up the roof pitches, and painting all the surfaces white, I was able to reveal the sculptural forms of the interior. Taking a step backwards, the architecture became a frame for viewing the landscape.

To showcase the incredible scenery, I chose wooden roman shades combined with sheer linen draperies that reinforced the pared-down aesthetic while artfully filtering the light. Into this setting, I introduced minimalist furnishings accented by jewel tones and colors inspired by the home's natural surroundings, interspersed with European antiques for warmth and character. Thick mohair and plush velvet ideal for the cool climate added tactile contrast.

PREVIOUS: When the range of a room's color is intentionally limited, texture can become a decisive factor. A rough mission-style cobble wall juxtaposed with a smooth limestone fireplace and a sleek lacquered coffee table enhance the tactile and visual energy of the living room. RIGHT: The absence of drapery allows the strength of the room's architecture to shine. Although the color palette is monochromatic, a variety of fabrics including silk velvet, linen, and wool add sensuous appeal. NEXT: Cantilevered from a mirrored panel and illuminated by crystal-and-brass sconces, the powder room's heavy marble sink appears to hover like a cloud.

Light can be the most important thing in a room. I deliberately invite it in through windows and allow it to reflect in different ways against the architecture and furnishings. Then, the play of light becomes a work of art all on its own. Excessive decoration can detract from this beautiful gift of nature, but restraint and order allow it quite literally to shine. In a family room in Virginia with northwest exposure, I omitted drapery from the tall, arched windows and French doors. This permitted natural light to bathe the stone fireplace wall, antique wool rug, lacquered coffee table, and silk velvet swivel chairs, modifying their textures and sheens and casting shifting shadows throughout the day.

I typically select a single powerful material, such as dramatically veined marble in an arresting color, and let that be the star in a kitchen or bathroom. I will surround it with complementary elements for texture and contrast, but avoid introducing another stone that would compete or distract from its individuality. When I designed a floating sink of Calacatta marble for a powder bath, it became a sculptural focal point. Despite their meticulous detailing, a full-length mirror inset into intricate wood paneling and brass accents played a supporting role. An approach of overall subtlety has its place, as well. In a neutral interior, varying the tonal relationships among objects while combining different fabrics and textures introduces depth. When you layer matte wool, cast glass, and raw silk with high-gloss finishes, polished nickel, or brushed oak, you can evoke an atmosphere of vibrancy and warmth.

I also believe in the potential of complementary color combinations to establish simplicity.

Once I upholstered every wall of an office nook with a vibrant, blue-and-white floral fabric, using it even for the window's shade. I chose a corresponding tone of blue to lacquer all the cabinetry and trim. Employed as a staple for the small space, the boldly patterned fabric became both focal point and backdrop for a colorful impressionist painting, polished nickel hardware, and an intricately woven rattan chair. Or take, for example, a powder room with brass-riveted, charcoal-gray wallpaper, mink-brown baseboards and moldings, a mirror with antiqued silvering, and fixtures with aged-metal finishes in tones of gray, brown, and black. Amid these sensuous materials, a white concrete sink with sharp geometric lines provided the necessary negative space. The final impression was one of handsome order. If you refrain from relying on the shock value of bright hues or busy patterns to carry the design, then the textures and forms of furnishings and architecture can realize strong, yet understated potential.

Our perceptions of a room should not only be about the design elements it contains—these alone are not intended to be what delight us. I believe in letting the feel and function of the room feed the spirit. Real beauty is found in discerning the heart of what matters to the people who abide within its walls. When we examine with introspection the source of our fulfillment, we may find that it is not a lifestyle crowded with excess possessions, but rather one graced by simple pleasures—an awe-inspiring view, a painting discovered on a recent trip, or the laughter of loved ones around a cozy breakfast table. By untangling our homes from the busyness of modern life, we can refocus on the true values that nourish our souls.

This remodeled home near Washington, DC, was transformed from an ornate, European chateau to a modern abode for an active young family. Fussy decor elements were replaced by crisp white walls and an organic palette, creating an inviting sanctuary for comfortable gatherings. In an era where open floor plans are the norm, this dwelling endorses rooms scaled to specific functions that create cozy, approachable environments. **OPPOSITE:** In the dining room, understated Belgian linen drapery and slipcovered chairs soften an alder table with chiseled metal legs. An oversize vintage rug underfoot is counterbalanced by a sleek, globed light fixture overhead.

ABOVE AND RIGHT: In the kitchen and breakfast room, pale oak beams and cabinetry offer contrast to the white-painted walls and ceilings. A custom banquette sofa nestles into a bay of windows. The oval table with a crossed-iron base provides a welcoming place for family meals and children's craft projects. Reclaimed oak beams frame the entrance from the kitchen to the adjacent family room.

OPPOSITE: Posed beneath an achromatic painting, a chest of rugged, aged wood immediately injects warmth and character into the formal living room. A pair of brushed-oak, barrel-back chairs carries out the organic theme. ABOVE: At the opposite end of the room, hand-formed ceramic sound bowls arranged on a wall become a three-dimensional work of art. Loose linen cushions and a medley of pillows give the sofa a casual silhouette, offset by the geometric lines of a cylindrical drink table and grid-backed accent chair.

ABOVE: In the dining room, the darkened legs of the table, a series of framed engravings, bronze drapery hardware, a collection of blackened clay pottery, and a quilted pillow punctuate their white surroundings.

ABOVE: A country French-style desk and linen armchair fit perfectly beneath the gabled roofline of the second-floor landing. NEXT: In the master bedroom, a soaring vaulted ceiling sets the stage for understated furnishings including the fully upholstered bed, leather bench, and grisaille driftwood sculptures. In the adjoining sitting room, a matte linen sofa sits atop a furry alpaca rug.

The design of this house expresses the homeowners' desire for a simple yet well-articulated environment that blurs the lines between indoor and outdoor spaces. With a focus on the interplay of negative and positive space, rooms become sculptural in character. While steel windows and polished concrete floors speak in a modern tongue, subtly expressed details define interiors that feel refined, inviting, and approachable. **OPPOSITE:** The kitchen's surfaces demonstrate a wide spectrum of light-reflecting properties, ranging from matte plaster and painted cabinetry to glossy countertops and frosted glass. **NEXT:** With double islands and a broad table, the kitchen and adjoining breakfast room are the heart of this home. Plaster, polished concrete, hand-molded subway tile, and iron upper cabinets unite in a seamless gray-and-white palette warmed by the breakfast table's wood tones.

ABOVE: With grid-like paneling that echoes the proportion of the windowpanes, the study conveys an atmosphere of calm and order. A painting of a peacock amid magnolia blooms relates the interior to the room's lush natural surroundings.

ABOVE: A nook enclosing a large gilt-framed mirror balances a doorway on the far side of the mantel to create an impression of symmetry. Natural materials including stained oak and chiseled limestone form a connection between the interior living space and adjacent patio.

OPPOSITE: In the breakfast room, expansive steel doors and windows blur the line between interior spaces and their exterior counterparts, emphasizing a bright, open plan. White leather-and-wood midcentury modern–style chairs offer smooth textures and clean lines that contrast with the table's rough, palette-like supports. BELOW: Situated beneath the shade of the patio's pergola, a rattan-style wingchair and ottoman and corresponding sofa form a relaxed room-like composition.

DEPTH

The interiors of our homes should be as rich and layered as life itself. They should be filled with meaningful treasures arranged in compositions that have nimbleness in their recipe and are never stilted nor static. The best interiors offer all who enter a discernible invitation to embrace life's gifts and to commune with the companions they share them with. They remind us to relish what is happening in the here and now and to savor cherished moments from the past. In our early-married years, my husband and I frequently took spontaneous road trips, stopping into small local shops along the way to search for unexpected jewels. One Saturday, I found a collection of antique keys that I eventually mounted on linen and displayed in white frames as a collage on the wall of my study. Something about those rusted metal keys silhouetted against delicate linen seemed poignant and profound. Whenever I walked past them, they unlocked a happy nostalgia about that time in our life. I understand now that they embodied my design philosophy even before I fully recognized it.

To this day, my aesthetic is exemplified by subtle contrasts of textures and finishes and unanticipated juxtapositions. I like for a room to feel ageless, as if it has been there for years. When all the materials match, a room feels contrived, but when there is dialogue among the polished and the honed, the matte and the glossy, the aged and the new, character deepens. Folding in authentic, organic materials and handcrafted objects enhances the spirit of a space. Whether newly designed or antique, I usually prefer to show things in their natural form. I gravitate toward reclaimed architectural antiques: vintage brass hardware, salvaged oak paneling, oxidized copper lanterns, or a reclaimed stone fireplace. When the inherently imperfect nature of such things is paired with streamlined contemporary furnishings, crisply tailored upholstery, and modern materials and finishes, a beautiful paradox is born that speaks to both the left and right sides of the brain.

A heightened awareness of their individual properties is awakened when seemingly opposing things are placed in proximity, as in an entry hall I designed where contemporary steel doors and windows flanked a distressed table with traditional forms. Immediately upon seeing this, the eye observed a broad span of time periods, origins, and aesthetics that managed to convey a single, cohesive statement. In the adjoining living room, the ornate forms of an antique stone mantel and gilded frame entered into conversation with the sleek arc of a contemporary sofa. Displayed amongst the precise framework of the room's coffered ceiling and pale stone floors, timeworn objects like a bronze ewer perched on a geometric pedestal found full expression. In situations where evidence of disparate eras coexists with modern environs, the sophistication of what has come before is made new again.

Color affords infinite opportunities to intensify the experience of being in a room. In a bedroom where plaster walls and a groin-vaulted ceiling formed a chalky backdrop, I introduced deep, saturated colors with duskier shades of charcoal, ochre, rust, and aubergine to devise an atmosphere that was at once intimate and dramatic. Pattern instantly conveys both movement and order. For a study in the same home, I combined a wood floor with an intricate pattern of alternating boards of walnut and oak with a shallow, coffered ceiling of stained walnut.

Dark paneling and bookcases of distressed ebonized wood heightened the graphic energy of the space, while also bestowing a slightly mysterious mood. To soften the effect, I added a lush, structured sofa upholstered in white raw silk and bold, natural pattern in the form of a hair-on-hide zebra rug. When the architectural features of a room are thoughtfully interwoven with the unique qualities of different fabrics and materials, richness of visual and tactile stimulation is achieved.

Endless inspiration can be drawn from the world of nature, such as stone, metal, wood, wool, leather, and living things. Creatively composing from the earth's palette provides bounteous opportunities to celebrate and combine its range of tones and textures. In a kitchen, I combined vintage-inspired cabinets with glossy Prussian blue paint and brass framing against marble countertops with dramatic taupe-and-gray veining. The atmosphere invoked by this marriage of materials was at once cozy and contemporary. Antique checkerboard stone flooring, bronze fixtures, and copper pans hanging above the stove brought more warmth into the mix. In the master bath of this same home, I fitted plaster walls with patinaed silver plumbing and light fixtures and paired a gleaming copper-and-nickel tub with a rustic European antique wood stool. In most rooms, I incorporate something living. Whether a potted tree or fresh cut flowers, nothing enlivens a space more than pulling something from outside the windows inside our walls.

I like to cultivate that same connectedness between what's outside and inside into the architecture of a home. Translating architectural elements from the exterior into the interior imbues a space with greater depth and dimension, indicating that a room is not just a shell of veneers. When a ceiling is vaulted to the true line of the roof ridge, the room expands into the full volume of the architectural envelope and assumes a feeling of magnitude and grandeur. In one project, I carried the stained-oak ceiling paneling of the porch into the adjoining living room, with a thin, steel window frame as the only division. In another, I wrapped the chopped-face limestone and smeared mortar of the exterior around to an interior wall, where it offered an arresting textural contrast to a sleek, cast-stone mantel and became the focal point of the room.

There is artistry and careful balancing involved in choosing elements that will complement one another without veering into chaos. It is beneficial to keep returning to the holistic rules established at the beginning of the design process regarding materials, finishes, colors, and other basic parameters. The choices and relationships established at the start become the cords that tie the whole design together in the end. By working with—and sometimes against—these guides, you can find endlessly creative ways to craft a deep and meaningful interior that will stand the test of time.

With many rooms opening with glass walls to private courtyards, this house benefits from a steady progression of light that enhances the beauty, simplicity, and richness of its materials. Marrying the earthy finishes of a Provençal manor with pared down classical forms and a minimalist color palette, the home's architecture and appointments forge a perfect balance between comfort and elegance. **PAGE 186**: With floor-to-ceiling walls of steel-framed glass, the foyer creates an airy impression balanced by the solidity of a limestone floor and substantial pedestal table. **PAGE 189**: Dark purple-and-gold orchids add the finishing touch to a fireside vignette. **PREVIOUS**: Dark walnut paneling adds dimension to one end of the living room, balancing the impact of the black-lacquered screen on the opposing wall. **OPPOSITE**: Checkerboard paving comprised of French limestone runs throughout the first floor rooms, adding weight and visual depth. Walls and ceilings of white plaster and diaphanous drapery lighten the effect.

ABOVE: A lacquered screen with gold-leaf details sets the living room's color story. Art deco–inspired chairs and rich upholstery fabrics highlight the room's nuanced shades.

ABOVE: The gentle curves and slate-blue linen of the breakfast chairs diversify the room's linear architecture. An age-darkened painting of a horse draws the eye in.

PREVIOUS: A limestone hood becomes part of this barrel-vaulted kitchen's architecture. OPPOSITE: An elliptical chandelier of gilt-lined mercury glass follows the oval lines of the dining room. ABOVE: Complex applications of wood cover the walls, floor, and ceilings of the library, where a zebra hide introduces additional pattern and a silk sofa becomes an island of calm.

ABOVE: An intricate antique mirror, milking bench with hoof-shaped feet, and Oushak carpet bring warm tones and varied materials into a monochromatic bathroom. The glossy tub and polished nickel hardware accentuate the matte character of the surrounding plaster and limestone. RIGHT: A minimalist color palette is expressed with maximal texture in a bedroom with gauzy linen hangings, an antiqued-velvet headboard, a nineteenth-century mirror, and contemporary metallic lamp.

BELOW: Inspired by one of the client's favorite classic movies, custom doors with an antique finish and bronze doorknobs add drama to the master suite's entrance. The paneled vestibule offers a moment of shadow and compression before opening to the luminous, vaulted bedroom. OPPOSITE: Countering the soaring effect of the bedroom's ceiling, a folding screen of walnut hugs the bed and side tables. Within the strong, masculine architecture of the room, a petite gilded Italian mirror provides a feminine touch.

OPPOSITE: A circular pendant echoes the shape of the tub beneath it, illuminating its reflective copper-and-tin contours. Natural light pours in through the arched picture window and bounces off the rococo mirror. ABOVE: A barrel-vaulted ceiling defines a hall-like passage that unites the bathroom's different spaces. The marble floor is peppered with black cabochons cut from the same slabs that enwrap the rift-cut oak vanities.

Constructed in the early 1900s, this Texas farmhouse was fully restored and updated to meet modern standards of beauty and comfort while also honoring its architectural heritage. Original flooring, moldings, and bead-board paneling were faithfully retained. Stacked and painted planks were used to dress new walls in a traditional way, forming a backdrop that skews both modern and historical. **OPPOSITE**: The organic form of a chair crafted from a tree root, weathered surfaces of an antique table, and French gilt-wood bench join in a sculptural composition.

LEFT: In the kitchen, soapstone counters and backsplashes, an oak island, and heavy wood beams lend a relaxed out-in-the-country mood. Seeded-glass pendants and the clients' collection of copper pans deliver gleaming reflections above, while an island with open shelves keeps dishes accessible below. ABOVE: In the butler's pantry, crisply tailored cabinetry painted a deep shade of blue paired with softly veined marble creates an interlude of urbane sophistication within the rustic surroundings.

ABOVE: In the dining room, an antique sideboard that gracefully reveals its age repeats the accents of blue that enrich the home's simple palette. Gilt-framed intaglios and mirrored sconces produce an elegant effect, balanced by the more utilitarian style of copper pendants.

ABOVE: Green velvet drapery reminiscent of *Gone with the Wind* adds a touch of romance to the bedroom, where an antique vanity mirror imitates the curves of the headboard.

BELOW AND OPPOSITE: The master bath is rich in historical charm expressed by the original bead-board ceiling, painted plank walls, and traditional patterned tile floor. Contemporary elements including steel doors and black-lacquered mirrors balance the old-fashioned claw-foot tub and dual vanity made from a vintage dresser.

SURPRISE

Each and every one of us has a distinct, original trait that expresses our personality and marks our identity. It might be the way we laugh or the quirk of an eyebrow that makes us unique and unforgettable. We all need something like this in our homes as well—a feature that establishes an unmistakable quality of individuality. It might be a striking painting or sculpture. Perhaps it is a floating staircase that appears to levitate upward through a serene entrance hall or an object so exquisitely crafted from extraordinary material that it inspires wonder. When interior design follows all the rules of convention, it is easy to feel detached, like an observer permitted only to experience a space or object at arm's length. Once something curious and whimsical is introduced, however, we are invited to participate firsthand. While a perfectly executed home attests to the designer's capability, a hint of surprise affirms that he or she was not so rigid as to relinquish spontaneity. Breaking the rules is what keeps design fresh and pushes us beyond the complacence of the expected.

I constantly challenge myself to look at things in new ways. My aim is to create eloquently poised, articulated spaces that are deliberately laced with eye-catching moments of color and scale and unconventional pairings of material and finish. These moments of surprise may be grand gestures that suggest a paradigm shift or be so understated that they only register in the subconscious. To be noticed, surprise doesn't have to be announced loudly. It can come through subtle sensory experiences: the scent of fresh flowers in a sitting room, the cool crispness of fine linens in the bedroom, or the calming sound of breezes wafting past an open window. A home's luxuries can be disclosed in a myriad of unanticipated ways, expanding the mind to new possibilities.

An element of surprise shouldn't be a strident thing that takes up all the air in a room. It should be a complementary presence that enhances what's already been done. When letting my imagination run off leash, I always remain mindful of the timeless principles of design, avoiding anything that interrupts harmony and balance. In a kitchen, which is typically focused on function, I might add an art ledge with colorful paintings that offers a moment devoted solely to aesthetic contemplation. For a bathroom, I might select lavishly veined slab marble in a saturated tone to cover multiple surfaces, not just as the countertop, but also a surround for the mirror, windows, and door casings. As a rule, illumination in bathrooms comes from wall fixtures, but if you dress the lavatory with table lamps, an atmosphere of coziness is invoked. Because we are more familiar with seeing task lighting in bathrooms, lamps might at first seem out of context. Finding them so attractively displayed in a powder bath might make us wonder why we had never thought to use them in such a setting before.

Pushing the limits of scale and material adds excitement to a design. Once, I repurposed an enormous antique vessel of roughly tumbled limestone, paired with a mirror with irregular antiqued silvering, as a lavatory sink in a powder room. An oversize light fixture instantly creates drama and establishes a compelling focal point. For a study with walls covered in an emerald-colored suede fabric and a grid-like coffered ceiling, I chose a hand-forged metal light fixture with undulating tendrils to hang in the room's center.

PAGE 214: A hand-painted mural of exuberant leaves and flowers festoons the walls of this dining room. PREVIOUS: A chandelier brings undulating organic forms into a study featuring mossy-green suede wallpaper that wraps over the edges of the ceiling. ABOVE: Walls can be treated as blank canvases awaiting unexpected details like the plaster-cast dogwood branches that reach across the walls of this bathroom.

Serving as both chandelier and artwork, it provided an almost startling organic contrast to the room's serious palette and orderly architecture. In a breakfast room, I installed a polished nickel ceiling fixture with exaggeratedly long arms, designed by Serge Mouille, to unite the seating group below and inject kinetic energy into the space. Fireplaces also offer prime opportunities to amplify scale. When you employ the monumental proportions of antique wood- or hand-carved stone mantels large enough to stand inside, they command attention and issue an invitation to gather near.

Some places have an inherent quality of mystery, folly, or private delight. I haven't met anyone yet who doesn't love a secluded window seat, a secret passage, a concealed silver cabinet, or an area set aside solely for painting, arranging flowers, or wrapping gifts. Even laundry rooms can become special spaces that are a pleasure to spend time in. When fitted with a deep sink of soapstone intended for cutting and arranging flowers, as well as copious counter space for household projects, a laundry room I designed for a client became a place where she loved to linger. Master bathrooms in which we inevitably spend time each morning and night should also be designed with an eye for unusual detail. For one, I commissioned an artist to create three-dimensional plaster flowers and vines that spread across a plaster wall painted the same white tone. Throughout the day, the light danced across their delicate forms, turning the entire room into an ever-changing work of art.

Master closets should also be beguiling, inviting us to escape there with a cocktail while dressing for the evening or for a second cup of coffee in preparation for the day. When each item is carefully displayed, a closet can become a place to rediscover our wardrobe, as if we are seeing it for the first time in a boutique. Opulent touches like doors of metal-wrapped antique mirrors that showcase formal gowns or handbag collections marry function with glamour. Creatively reimagining materials not usually associated with small spaces—leather-wrapped panels, large-patterned wallpaper, or brass-inlaid millwork—can make each closet or dressing room more personal and satisfying.

I love taking risks and am in awe of the trust my clients have invested in me over the years. Almost always, the one aspect that seemed the most daring becomes our favorite part of the project. After clients permitted me to install checkerboard flooring of two types of limestone across the entire ground level of their home, we were elated by the simultaneously dramatic and understated way it united all the spaces. With each out-of-the-box venture, I stretch my comfort zone and invite my clients to do the same. Who wants to live in a house that doesn't enthrall them a little bit every time they come back to it? If we are not stirred by the thrill of seeing a project come to life, we are not challenging ourselves enough.

Surprise speaks to us because we universally thirst for adventure and opportunities to step outside the ordinariness of everyday life and into a world of new possibilities and amazement. In our homes, we hope for delight on a daily basis that will awaken us to the beauty of the present moment and prompt us to rejoice in our surroundings. When something unanticipated and even astonishing is thoughtfully integrated into the overall experience of a space, it reminds us that life is full of unexpected joy and discovery. This is the beauty of home.

BELOW: A crimson onyx vanity floating on a wall of dark gray plaster becomes the element of surprise in this powder room, where a curvaceous, carved gilt-wood mirror adds another unexpected touch. OPPOSITE: In a bedroom, a hand-painted scene of flowering trees executed on pieced and lightly antiqued paper creates the impression of being in a walled garden.

PREVIOUS: Multiple accent pieces harmonize in the all-white envelope of the living room, including an aubergine arced sofa, an antique capital, a spool-legged table, a classical ewer, and a fifteenth-century, Dante-style chair. An antique mirror with glass blackened by age resembles a contemporary work of art. OPPOSITE: A tightly defined space like a study or media room presents the perfect situation for a spirited statement. In this room, dark green cabinetry with grass-cloth backing forms a geometric surround for a sofa with an even livelier geometric pattern. ABOVE: The rustic carving of bleached-oak doors and an Indian wood-and-leather bench serve as foils for the lustrous sheen of an elegant tufted-velvet headboard. The bold grain of the solid-wood bedside table brings organic energy and modern edge into the composition.

BELOW: Layers upon layers of detail define this master bathroom, where a cubist painting hangs against a ribbed-glass shower wall. The interplay between the heavily veined marble floor and walls with a caned midcentury modern chair and accompanying towel stand brings more dynamic contrast to the space. OPPOSITE: Petite bathrooms are ideal places for dramatic wall coverings like this oversize black-and-white palm motif.

ABOVE: A sizable carved-stone planter becomes a dramatic vessel sink, the focal point of this powder room. Graphite-colored walls and an antiqued mirror emphasize its earthy tone and rugged texture. RIGHT: Within this study, the graphic pattern and bold colors of a hand-knotted carpet unites disparate items that express a collected sensibility.

LEFT: A pleated-silk headboard is an unexpectedly lavish interlude among the bedroom's modernist cabinets and white-on-white walls. Subtle artwork by Agnes Martin manifests the poised minimalism of the surroundings. ABOVE: Displayed in a mixture of frame styles, works representing a variety of mediums animate this office space. The irregular outline of layered hide rugs balance the graphically arranged collection.

ABOVE: Floor-to-ceiling drapery and tall sconces above a French-style stone mantel magnify the sheer volume of the master bedroom's vaulted oak ceiling. Beneath the delicate crystal pendants of the chandelier, a cowhide rug brings the design down to earth.

ABOVE: Reaching out over a pair of contemporary bronze chairs, a monumental, carved-limestone fireplace envelops the seating area. Distinct characters like the spiraling chandelier, arched steel doors, and unconventional floor lamp energize the room.

OPPOSITE: Gleaming brass hardware and a purposefully oversize pendant light endow this bar area with graphic appeal. The softer form of an arched window deeply beveled into plaster introduces a historical touch. ABOVE: The standout feature in this powder room is a carved-plaster mural with gold and silver leaf details by artist John Opella. Taking cues from its palette, the vanity pairs charcoal-painted cabinetry with a celadon quartzite countertop.

RIGHT: A low-slung sofa and slipper chairs upholstered with lamb's wool amplify the height of the living room's ceiling. Abstract art by Claire Oswalt sets the blue-and-white palette for the room, balancing the more traditional statements of a painted mirror and graceful Dutch-style chandelier. NEXT: Within this living room's subdued palette of black, brown, and gray, strong players like a gilded-and-painted klismos chair and abstract painting by Mary Case with marble vein–like markings create a striking composition.

ACKNOWLEDGMENTS

Volumes could be written to contain the names of those who have shared this journey toward the beauty of home. This book would not exist without the vision and talent of so many. To the homeowners who shared this journey, thank you for entrusting me with what you hold most dear. It is a privilege to dream and collaborate with each of you.

Countless individuals have brought their creative energy to this endeavor. These include my staff of designers: Melanie Hamel, Sydney Manning, Ashlee Garner, Kristin Amundsen, and Kelsey Grant, who also gave hours of feedback and advice toward this book; Julie DiPaolo, who works tirelessly to make our creations become reality; Rachel Manning, Michaela Williams, Kristen Emerson, Jennifer Hammer, and many more who have been a part of my team throughout the years. I am deeply grateful for each person's willingness to conquer any challenge.

I have had the honor to work alongside some of the finest architects, builders, craftsmen, and landscape architects of our time. It truly would not be possible to realize our design visions without them, and I am humbled to represent their workmanship in these pages and the resource guide.

It is the skill of exceptional photographers that breathes life into two-dimensional pictures, translating them in a captivating way for a wider audience. I cannot thank principle photographer, Julie Soefer, as well as Claudia Casbarian and Rachel Manning, enough for the expertise and artistry they brought to the images included here. Much appreciation also goes to Jessica Brinkert Holtam, whose meticulous styling enhanced every room she touched.

Much gratitude goes to my editor at Gibbs Smith, Katie Killebrew, for believing in this project years before I was willing to, and to graphic designer, Jan Derevjanik, who brought order and beauty to the layouts. And finally, many thanks to coauthor, Susan Sully, who helped articulate the words on these pages and gave my life experiences a voice.

It is with all my love and gratitude that I dedicate this book to my husband, Joe, and our three children John, William, and Eve. Thank you for your unending love and support.

RIVER OAKS WEST

Designer: Marie Flanigan & Melanie Hamel
Marie Flanigan Interiors | www.marieflanigan.com
Architect: Reagan Miller, Andre DeJean & Michael Roeder
Reagan & Andre Architecture Studio | www.reaganandre.com
Builder: Barry Brown
Brownridge Builders | www.brownridgebuilders.com
Landscape Architect: Johnny Steele & Tracy Engle
Johnny Steele Design

BRIARGROVE PARK

Designer: Marie Flanigan
Marie Flanigan Interiors | www.marieflanigan.com
Architect: Sam Gianukos
Creole Design | www.creoledesign.com
Builder: David Weekley Homes
www.davidweekleyhomes.com

RIVER OAKS CENTRAL

Designer: Marie Flanigan
Marie Flanigan Interiors | www.marieflanigan.com
Architect: Travis Mattingly
Architectural Solutions, Inc. | www.asi-design.com
Builder: Overstreet Builders
www.overstreet-builders.com

HUNTERS CREEK

Designer: Marie Flanigan & Sydney Manning
Marie Flanigan Interiors | www.marieflanigan.com
Architect: Rodney Stevens & Thomas Cook
Frankel Building Group | www.frankelbuildinggroup.com
Builder: James Milford, Scott Frankel & Brian Adams
Frankel Building Group | www.frankelbuildinggroup.com
Landscape Architect: Johnny Steele
Johnny Steele Design

BUNKER HILL

Designer: Marie Flanigan & Rachel Anderson
Marie Flanigan Interiors | www.marieflanigan.com
Architect: Brick Moon Design
www.brickmoondesign.com
Builder: Erin Stetzer
Stetzer Builders | www.stetzerbuilders.com

TELLURIDE

Designer: Marie Flanigan & Alyse Harrison
Marie Flanigan Interiors | www.marieflanigan.com
Builder: J&S Richardson Construction

MARBLE FALLS

Designer: Marie Flanigan & Melanie Hamel
Marie Flanigan Interiors | www.marieflanigan.com
Builder: Zbranek and Holt Custom Homes
www.zhcustomhomes.com
Landscape Architect: Michael J. Logsdon
Land Design Texas | www.landdesigntx.houzz.com

GALVESTON

Designer: Marie Flanigan & Kelsey Grant
Marie Flanigan Interiors | www.marieflanigan.com
Builder: Douglas LeBoeuf
LeBoeuf Homes, Inc. | www.leboeufhomes.com

BRIARGROVE SOUTH

Designer: Marie Flanigan & Ashlee Garner
Marie Flanigan Interiors | www.marieflanigan.com
Architect: Kelly Cusimano & Luis Salcedo
Cusimano Architect | www.cusimano-architect.com
Builder: Erin Stetzer
Stetzer Builders | www.stetzerbuilders.com
Landscape Architect: Teresa Villa
Teresa Villa Designs
Landscape Architect: Tom Read
Prewett, Read & Associates | www.prewettread.com

MEMORIAL PARK

Designer: Marie Flanigan, Kelsey Grant & Sydney Manning
Marie Flanigan Interiors | www.marieflanigan.com
Builder: Brian Cronin
Cronin Builders | www.croninbuilders.com

MCLEAN

Designer: Marie Flanigan & Kelsey Grant
Marie Flanigan Interiors | www.marieflanigan.com
Builder: Chris Heisey
Snead Custom Homes | www.sneadcustomhomes.com

BELLAIRE

Designer: Marie Flanigan & Melanie Hamel
Marie Flanigan Interiors | www.marieflanigan.com
Architect: Brad Hollenbeck
Hollenbeck Architects | www.hollenbeckarchitects.com
Builder: Philip Robbins
Bentley Custom Homes | www.bentleycustomhomes.com
Landscape Architect: Travis Peiffer
White Oak Studio | www.wos-la.com

MEMORIAL

Designer: Marie Flanigan & Sydney Manning
Marie Flanigan Interiors | www.marieflanigan.com
Architect: Kirby Mears, Walter Murphy & Sam Brisendine
Murphy Mears Architects | www.murphymears.com
Builder: Dirk Hoyt & Erich Kleine
University Towne Building Corporation | www.utbc.net

BRENHAM

Designer: Marie Flanigan & Alyse Harrison
Marie Flanigan Interiors | www.marieflanigan.com
Architect: Kelly Cusimano
Cusimano Architect | www.cusimano-architect.com
Builder: Walcik Construction
www.walcikconstruction.com